Enduring Themes in Educational Change

Enduring Themes in Educational Change

David A. Escobar Arcay

RESOURCE *Publications* • Eugene, Oregon

Enduring Themes in Educational Change

Resource Publications
An Imprint of Wipf and Stock Publishers
199 W. 8th Ave., Suite 3
Eugene, OR 97401

www.wipfandstock.com

PAPERBACK ISBN: 978-1-5326-0904-6
HARDCOVER ISBN: 978-1-5326-0906-0
EBOOK ISBN: 978-1-5326-0905-3

Manufactured in the U.S.A.   FEBRUARY 6, 2017

Contents

Overview

IF YOU ARE A researcher, educator, or reformer, and are not fully aware of the speed and amount of educational change that is intended and tried in today's public schools, then you will be fortunate and grateful to find many experts in the educational change process. However, you may find yourself bewildered by the voluminous publications (books and articles) and desire to have a quick read that will alert you to the core themes in the educational change literature. What if you can quickly learn the key operational concepts that undergird theories of educational change?

This book facilitates this learning by summarizing and describing some of the educational change themes that run throughout the works of Canadian scholar and theorist of educational change: Michael Fullan. It is important to note that this work does not constitute a biography (or intellectual biography for that matter) of said scholar. This work simply represents a personal reflection of various themes and a humble and modest attempt to provide professional educators an entry into the vast field of educational change. It is also important to note that this work is not a critical analysis of this scholar's works, but merely an exercise that is descriptive in nature. This book selects and examines these themes from his sixteen published (authored and coauthored) books from 1982 to 2008. It is a fact that this text may have serious limitations because of the restricted scope in years (1982 to 2008) of texts selected and the unquestioned and increasing evidence that this scholar's positions in some of these themes have developed significantly. The reader is reminded again that this work constitutes a basic and immediate entry way into the field of educational change. The reader is also challenged and invited to read and engage this scholar's works after 2008 to trace, underscore and denote changes (both continuities and discontinuities) in the predominant themes listed in this text which will surely may highlight and illuminate some of my shortcomings and weaknesses for which I, as the sole author, take full responsibility. The themes described in the present text consist of stakeholders in education (students, teachers, principals, parents and community, district administrators, and consultants); process; dimensions (the objective reality); assumptions (the subjective reality); moral purpose; relationships; knowledge; sustainability; complexity/chaos and evolutionary theory; systems; paradoxes; coherence; and theory of action. Each theme is immediately followed by a quote or two from selected texts.

It is important to note three things. First, singling out these themes in no way confirms that these themes are independent and/or unrelated to each other. Separating themes is a deliberate and conscious attempt on my part to address and organize some of the key ideas in the field of educational change. These themes are interdependent and feed on each other. Second, the descriptive nature of the themes provided here could be found or referenced in more than one book. Finally, these themes are listed here in no particular order of preference or importance.

1

Stakeholders

The People in Education

"Educational change is a process of coming to grips with the multiple realities of people, who are the main participants in implementing change. . . . Educational change, above all, is a people-related phenomenon for each and every individual."

—*The New Meaning of Educational Change, 96–97; 151.*

Students

"Integral to the argument of this chapter is that treating students as people comes very close to 'living' the academic, personal, and educational goals that are stated in most official policy documents. But more than that, involving students in constructing their own meaning and learning is fundamentally pedagogically essential—they learn more, and are motivated to go even further."

—*The New Meaning of Educational Change, 162.*

Innovations often become ends in themselves. Students become the means. For the most part, students are treated solely as the benefactors of innovations. They are passive, not active, participants in the process of change. The union of cognitive science and sociology may signal a renewed interest in the active role of students in educational changes.[1] It is essential to provide students opportunities for cognitive as well as emotional development. This provides the academic dimension plus the social dimension. It is about both motivation and relationships. It is ultimately an excellence and equity issue. A professional learning community is nurtured in ways that integrate the insights of those who seek to redefine schools and change the power relations that sustain the student achievement gap.

Most students report that teachers and principals do not understand their point of view, appreciate their opinions, or listen to them. Students appear to be alienated. Many students are highly passive in terms of the governance of the classroom. They are not considered or listened to when the teacher is making decisions about classroom management, planning, learning, and teaching. Students' voices, insights, and ideas need to be tapped as a resource to shape learning and teaching for productive educational change to take place.[2] An appropriate question here would be to ask to what extent the educational change literature has taken student voice into consideration.

Teachers

"We don't have a learning profession. Teachers and teacher educators do not know enough about

1. Michael Fullan, *The New Meaning of Educational Change*, third edition (New York: Teachers College Press, 2001).

2. Ibid.

subject matter, they don't know enough about how to teach, and they don't know enough about how to understand and influence the conditions around them. Above all, teacher education—from initial preparation to the end of the career—is not geared towards continuous learning."

—*Changing Forces: Probing the Depths of Educational Reform, 108.*

"Ultimately, what is important is the capacity of teachers—individually and with others—to manage change continuously. This means the ability to find meaning among an array of innovative possibilities, and to become adept at knowing when to seek change aggressively, and when to back off."

—*Successful School Improvement, 23.*

Our society fails teachers because it gives students failing grades and does not improve teachers' working conditions. The problem begins with teacher preparations programs, which lack internal as well as external coherence. There are insufficient induction programs for beginning teachers. The transitions of becoming a teacher, coupled with their problems in the management of instruction and feelings of loneliness and isolation, are documented as other sources in the poor preparation of teachers. Teaching in the inner city is one of the most stressful occupations. Teaching is not a learning profession yet. It is not geared toward continuous learning.

There is a strong need for teachers to grow through a process of personal development in a social context. There have been several attempts trying to remedy this problem, but they have proven to only scratch the surface. One of them was the Teacher Corps and Trainers of Teacher Trainers program.[3] This social change-based effort was described as merely a large-scale tinkering effort. It failed because it was a vague, individualistic, non-systemic, knowledge-less and only school-based program. Others included the strategies of the Education Commission States, which were effective.[4] However, in the long term they were doomed to failure because they did not take into account developing the capacity of the school or reculturing. Still, other efforts with an explicit social reconstructionist agenda were also doomed to failure because they were too ambitious. The issue here is that these attempts failed because they did not change schools into learning organizations.

Reforming teacher education requires the convergence of moral purpose and knowledge and skills development. Moral purpose needs to be part of the institutional objectives of teacher education. Teachers need to have the knowledge and skills to change institutions as well as to contend with forces of change in complex environments. There is also a strong need for developing an expanded knowledge and skill base that will allow teachers to not only teach a variety of individuals but also influence their working conditions. This expansion of roles and responsibilities mentioned here will not take place unless teacher knowledge is substantially improved.

Understanding teacher development implies providing opportunities for knowledge and skills development, self-understanding, and ecological change.[5] Professional development of educators is about developing habits of learning. The question here is what set of policies provide

3. Ibid.

4. Ibid.

5. Michael Fullan, *Successful School Improvement* (Buckingham: Open University Press, 1992).

teachers with opportunities to learn new ways for working while interacting with each other. Purposeful and focused collaboration needs to take place. Reculturing the entire profession means providing corresponding development mechanisms that are grounded in standards of practice, providing strategies embedded in the workplace, and identifying and strengthening leadership practices that focus continuously on the previous two factors.[6]

Scholars have suggested the following guidelines for teachers: "Locate, listen to and articulate your inner voice; practice reflection in action, on action and about action; develop an at-risk mentality; trust processes as well as people; appreciate the total person in working with orders; commit to working with colleagues; seek variety and avoid balkanization; redefine your role to extend beyond the classroom; balance work and life; push and support principals and other administrators to develop interactive professionalism; commit to continuous improvement and perpetual learning and monitor and strengthen the connection between your development and students' development."[7]

Principals

"To change schools we must change ourselves. More specifically, we must undergo a huge paradigm shift from, as they say in the university, being the dependent variable to becoming the independent variable."

—*What's Worth Fighting for in the Principalship?, vii.*

6. Michael Fullan, *Leading in a Culture of Change* (San Francisco: Jossey-Bass, 2001).

7. Fullan, *Successful School Improvement*, 64–83.

The conditions that govern the principalship demand radical change.[8] First, the principalship appears to be not very attractive due to the multiple demands of the job and the work overload that it fosters. Second, historically conservative tendencies in the principalship make matters worse. Teachers are narrowly prepared for the principalship. Many are prey to the undeniable pressures of maintaining and restoring stability. As a result, principals do not engage resistance in constructive ways but rather in silent opposition that allows it to take root. Third, many principals operate under more self-imposed conceptions of the systems than truly exist. The ways in which a principal views the system may exclude him from seeing a universe of alternatives that may bring many possibilities. Finally, the rational model has historically shaped and dominated the governance of institutions in the West. It is problematic and creates a sense of dependency among principals because it is based on the "if then, if only" philosophy and operates under the assumption that problems are easily explained and solved. This rational model compounds the situation because school systems are guided by multiple, competing goals; power is unequally distributed throughout the organization; decision making is inevitably a bargaining process to arrive at solutions that satisfy a number of constituencies; the public influences school systems in major ways that are unpredictable; and the effectiveness of teaching practices is heavily contested.

Modern management techniques are therefore full of limitations.[9] First, principals must start admitting that there is no silver bullet out there. Second, the leader must engage with the ideas in a real context in order to test those

8. Michael Fullan, *What's Worth Fighting for in the Principalship?*, first edition (New York: Teachers College Press, 1997).

9. Ibid.

management techniques and find out whether these help to solve the problems or exacerbate the situation. Third, the principal's work should be grounded in an entrepreneurial spirit and positive political skills. The changing structure of innovative organizations from tighter control to more flexible working conditions predicts and demands that middle managers (principals) may help their own sense of powerlessness by servicing, contributing to, and creating a climate or culture that helps those with whom they work. A principal's actions should be balanced between maintenance and greatness, caution and courage, and dependency and autonomy. Fourth, limited conceptions of leaders drive the system and are found in society's deep-seated notions of traditional leaders. The leader's job is to design a school culture or climate where people learn to deal with the issues that they face. His work is to listen to others to enhance the vision they bring and help synthesize his own vision with others to get a deeper and richer perspective on improvement and growth. This implies that the leader in a learning organization must deal with or navigate through polar opposites. The leader is responsible for acting in ways previously unknown. The changing role of principals in schools suggests that they should suspend advocacy and legitimize dissent, combine individual and collective effort with vision, and welcome the presence of parents and communities as an opportunity to shift power relations and arrangements.

Several guidelines for actions are provided for principals that are consistent with the new conceptions of leadership. These include the following: "avoid 'if only . . . statements'"; "start small, think big"; "don't over plan and over manage"; "focus on fundamentals: curriculum, instruction, assessment, professional culture"; "practice fearlessness"; "embrace diversity and resistance while empowering others"; "build a vision relevant to both goals and processes"; "decide what you are not going to do"; "build allies"; "know when to be cautious"; and, finally, "give up the search for the silver bullet."[10] Educational leaders can no longer operate under the old assumptions and/or mindset. "The principal is the key to creating the conditions for the continuous professional development of teachers and thus, of classroom and school improvement."[11]

Parents and the Community

> "Nowhere is the two-way street of learning more in disrepair and in need of social reconstruction than with concerning the relationship among parents, communities and their schools. Teachers and principals need to reach out to parents and communities, especially when the initial conditions do not support such efforts."
>
> —*The New Meaning of Educational Change, 198.*

Given the fact that the boundaries of the schools and the outside environment have become more blurry, it is therefore necessary that schools pay close attention to parents and communities.[12] Teachers, principals, and schools can no longer remain isolated from their immediate outside environments. Parental engagement in education leads to increased academic achievement. Teachers and principals need much help in connecting with parents and the community. However, parents and communities also need help

10. Ibid., 27.

11. Fullan, *Successful School Improvement*, 96.

12. Michael Fullan and A. Hargreaves, *What's Worth Fighting for Out There?* (New York: Teachers College Press, 1998).

in the development of those skills that can help them make a good contribution to their respective schools. Teachers, principals, and schools alike need to find and use parental involvement practices that will increase parents' understanding and knowledge about their children's instructional program.

The role of school boards should not be dismissed as unnecessary or counterproductive. School boards can make a difference when there is clarity about what is expected of them as well as the practices and programs that govern their respective districts. They can also make a difference when they establish activities purposely designed to strengthen the capacity of their districts based on district data and a set of common values. There is a strong need for a learning school board.

Nonetheless, due to the excessive number of reform policies to be implemented as well as the lack of attention that these have for effective institutionalization, it is advisable that the starting point should be parental engagement. A popular conception is that most parents are disengaged from their children. Training and development offered in local communities and neighborhoods for effective parent and school connections can help counter this trend. This could be school or community initiated. While it is true that in the past teachers and principals have either resisted making these connections or started connections that were superficial and did not last, parents are strongly advised to change their thinking in regard to advocacy for schools. Parents can "press governments to create the kind of teachers you want; leave nostalgia behind you; ask what you can do for your school as well as what your school can do for you and to put praise before blame."[13]

13. Ibid., 124–25.

District Administrators

> "It is possible for an individual school to become highly collaborative despite the district it is in, but it is not likely that it will stay collaborative. If the district does not foster professional learning communities by design, it undermines them by default. We now know that schools will not develop if left to their own devices."
>
> —*The New Meaning of Educational Change*, 165.

The changing role of the school superintendent represents a huge shift "away from the role of educational spokesperson and executive manager of a relatively homogeneous system, toward one where negotiation and conflict management of diverse interests and groups predominate."[14] District administrators are also viewed by the school as less than helpful. The cause is attributed to projects and their resulting debilitating effects in terms of both teacher and principal skepticism about latest reform efforts. In addition, district administrators overlook the big picture, thus creating an inconsistent and disconnected approach of district policies with school realities, especially in the eyes of principals.

What school districts need to counteract these problems is reculturing with an explicit and sustained focus on instruction, capacity, meaning, and coherence. District administrators have three tasks. First, the district administrator needs to "recognize and unleash the power they have to do good."[15] Second, there needs to be reculturing "toward interactive, accountable, inclusive professional learning

14. Fullan, *The New Meaning of Educational Change*, third edition, 166.

15. Ibid., 179.

communities."[16] Finally, the district administrator needs to "model learning."[17]

Consultants

> "It is clear that consultants providing service and those using it have a lot to learn. In general terms, what is needed is that external initiatives and those relating to them must base their work on both a high quality theory of learning and a high quality theory of action (or, if you like, a theory of pedagogy and a theory of change, which constantly feed on each other). A theory of pedagogy focuses on assumptions about learning, instruction, and performance; a theory of action tends to local context such as the conditions under which the model will work."
>
> —*The New Meaning of Educational Change, 187.*

In the culture of change that is present in our society and schools, the demand for help is inevitable. Our schools are invaded by a stream of innovations in collision with other innovations that may work in some but not all situations. School reform models that focus on both pedagogy and context produce greater student achievement. Promising models are guided by a strong theory-based change. Developing the conditions implied in the theory of change and action is the big challenge.

Consultancy represents a promise in relation to this challenge. External consultants can build capacity (and thus conditions) through the use of good ideas about learning

16. Ibid., 180.
17. Ibid., 182.

and by relating the model being implemented to the bigger picture of the many initiatives functioning around the district. External consultants could replicate the conditions that lead to the success of other school reform models when they focus on coherence and connectedness.

Principals and teachers considering using consultants should be careful when employing them. They should assess the extent to which external ideas or programs being presented have a theory of change that can address the process of implementation. They should also assess whether that external idea or program can be integrated with other ideas already put into action and closely monitor to what extent this idea or program is able to increase the knowledge and motivation of teachers.

2

Educational Process

"Educational change is a process, not an event."
— *The New Meaning of Educational Change, 52.*

THE CHANGE PROCESS HAS three phases.[1] These phases are initiation, mobilization, or adoption; implementation or initial use; and continuation, incorporation, routinization, or institutionalization. This is also known as the Triple I model. Initiation consists of the process "that leads up to and includes a decision to adopt or proceed with a change."[2] Implementation involves "the first experiences of attempting to put an idea or reform into practice."[3] Institutionalization refers to "whether the change gets built in as an ongoing part of the system or disappears by way of a decision to discard or through attrition."[4] These three phases are to be evaluated in terms of whether or not the outcomes of student learning and the capacity of the school as an institution were attained and enhanced respectively. The change process is complicated due to the presence of

1. Ibid.
2. Ibid., 50.
3. Ibid., 50.
4. Fullan, *Leading in a Culture of Change*, 50.

many factors, such as its nonlinear nature, the scope of the project, the source of the change, as well as the historical context.

Many factors operate at each phase. The initiation phase is affected by the following: existence and quality of innovations; access to innovations; advocacy from central administration; teacher advocacy; external change agents; community pressure or support/apathy; federal, state, and local funding; and problem solving and bureaucratic orientations.[5] The implementation phase includes characteristics of change, such as need, clarity, complexity, and quality/practicality; local characteristics, such as the district, community, principal, and teacher; and other external factors, such as government and other agencies. Factors crucial for institutionalization include active leadership, professional development, and the support or neglect of the larger infrastructure. In addition, there are four problems that interact with this Triple I model. These are the challenges of including numerous people in the process; combining pressure and support; the changing of behavior and beliefs (in which people experience an "implementation dip"); and the role of ownership.

Educational change is a process, not an event. It is a process mediated by more than one factor resulting in a number of problems that should be readily anticipated and addressed by reformers if the change process is to be successful.

---

5. Fullan, *The New Meaning of Educational Change*, third edition.

3

Dimensions

The Objective

"The difficulty is that educational change is not a single entity even if we keep the analysis at the simplest level of an innovation in a classroom. Innovation is multidimensional."

—*The New Meaning of Educational Change, 39.*

THE MULTIDIMENSIONALITY OF EDUCATIONAL change is characterized by three components or dimensions. These are described as, first, "the possible use of new or revised materials (instructional resources such as curriculum materials or technologies)"; second, the possible use of "new teaching approaches (i.e., new teaching strategies or activities)"; and, third, the possible "alteration of beliefs (e.g., pedagogical assumptions and theories underlying particular new policies or programs)."[1] The attempted or initiated change must take place in practice along these three dimensions. However, it is possible that a teacher's work touch upon one dimension while neglecting others.

1. Ibid., 39.

This objective reality of change faces three difficulties.[2] The first difficulty refers to the originating source of these dimensions, or, to put it another way: who says what approaches, beliefs, and materials are to be implemented, altered, and used respectively? The tension between the fidelity and mutual adaptation or evolutionary perspective is the second difficulty. The fidelity perspective is "based on the assumption that an already developed innovation exists and the task is to get individuals and groups of individuals to implement it faithfully in practice."[3] On the other hand, the mutual adaptation or evolutionary perspective "stresses that change often is (and should be) a result of adaptations and decisions made by users as they work with particular new policies or programs, with the policy or program and the user's situation mutually determining the outcome."[4] The third difficulty lies in the fact that it is very hard to define what is to be changed. This is because as an initiative is implemented there is further transformation, modification, and development. However, at the same time, it will be appropriate and valuable to attempt to define what is to be changed due to the fact that there is an inherent need in knowing whether things have changed.

The possibilities for real change along these three dimensions lie in addressing them on a "continuous basis through communities of practice"[5] and in keeping in mind that beliefs can be unpacked after people have had some interaction with the new practices being attempted.

2. Ibid.

3. Ibid., 40.

4. Ibid., 4.

5. Michael Fullan, *The Moral Imperative of School Leadership* (Thousand Oaks, Ca.: Corwin, 2003), 45.

4

Assumptions

The Subjective

"Educational change fails partly because of the
assumptions of planners, and partly because
solving substantial problems is an inherently
complex business. . . . The fallacy of rationalism
is the assumption that the social world can be
altered by logical argument. The problem, as
George Bernard Shaw observed, is that 'reformers have the ideas that change can be achieved
by brute sanity.'"

—*The New Meaning of*
Educational Change, 96, 98.

EDUCATIONAL CHANGE FAILS BECAUSE of the assumptions
underlying its rational, contextual, and cultural insensitiv-
ity and seductive appeal and nature.[1] First, the fact that a
principal or teacher is committed to a certain educational
initiative does not guarantee that this person knows how
that initiative is to be implemented. Change is not a rational
process. The fallacy of rationalism is to be blamed for the
failure of planning. Competing versions of the purposes,

1. Fullan, *The New Meaning of Educational Change*, third edition.

17

goals, or outcomes of educational changes defeat any notion of rationality. The tendency to assume that the world can be changed by a logical argument is merely wishful thinking given the presence of many voices who claim to have the right version of that change.

Second, educational change fails because it is insensitive to the local context and culture. Failure occurs because the focus is on the initiative rather than on the structures, conditions, and norms that are crucial for a change to flourish. This explains why resistance to change should be treated as a source of learning. Resisters may have some good ideas. Neglecting their concerns may block further implementation.

Finally, educational change fails because of its seductive appeal and/or nature. Facing multiple and colliding demands, a principal or teacher may opt to go with a simple checklist. It may be easy and more comfortable to rely on gurus or adopt so-called experts' management techniques. It may be comfortable and relaxing to know that someone is in control or that you are part of a great plan—a plan in which, if you only follow some vision, then everything will fall into place. This thinking and mindset may create and nurture dependency and false certainty.

5

Moral Purpose

"Moral purpose of the highest order is having a
system where all students learn, the gap between
high and low performance becomes greatly re-
duced, and what people learn enables them to
be successful citizens and workers in a morally
based society."

—*The Moral Imperative of*
School Leadership, 29.

"Managing moral purpose and change agentry
is at the heart of productive educational change."

—*Changing Forces: Probing the Depths of*
Educational Reform, 8.

MORAL PURPOSE IS ABOUT the improvement of educa-
tion for all students and about knowing how to get there.
Pursuing moral purpose in a culture of change is complex.
One case in point was the National Literacy and Numeracy
Strategy in England.[1] This large-scale governmental initia-
tive aimed to increase the achievement of children up to

1. Fullan, *Leading in a Culture of Change*; *The New Meaning of*
Educational Change, third edition.

eleven years old in the areas of literacy and math. This national attempt to raise achievement was driven by moral purpose because it was an explicit attempt at making a difference in the lives of students. It provided practical strategies and action steps for accomplishing its achievement targets. The motives of many stakeholders—such as teachers, principals, or the government—were advanced. Finally, it triggered the question of what was the right purpose and the route towards intrinsic commitment.

However, moral purpose does not necessarily lead people to do good things all the time.[2] Moral purpose is problematic because it must struggle to reconcile different voices that express different values, goals, and purposes. It is evolutionary. Its potential must be somehow triggered and nurtured in order to flourish. In the world of education, educators are fusing the spiritual, emotional, and intellectual in their careers and workplaces. In the business world, companies are expected to have a social conscience or soul. Moral purpose and performance are mutually dependent and cannot be treated as if they are unrelated or as if society could have one at the expense of the other.

Moral purpose is now part of the restructuring movement, such as when schools are designed in ways to allow the participation of those groups of students that have been historically marginalized. Moral purpose is the building block of the individual teacher.[3] However, moral purpose at the interpersonal level is seen as limited unless it is redefined to address the broader social conditions that affect teaching. It is about linking this moral purpose and personal care to a broader social agenda grounded in the skills of change agentry. Educators must accompany their moral

2. Fullan, *Leading in a Culture of Change.*

3. Michael Fullan, *Change Forces: Probing the Depths of Educational Reform* (London: Falmer, 1993).

purpose with knowledge about how to engage in change. They need to be agents of change. Change agentry is about "being self-conscious about the nature of change and the change process."[4]

To enact change, teachers need four core capacities: personal vision building, inquiry, mastery, and collaboration. The institutional counterparts of these teacher capacities are shared vision building, organizational structures, norms, and practices of inquiry; focus on organizational development; and know-how and collaborative work cultures. A dual approach is in place—individual and institutional development. Personal purpose and vision building imply that educators must ask themselves why they came into the profession and what is important to them. Inquiry demands that educators adopt a process of questioning as the answer. Mastery is more than just becoming an expert at applying what one has learned. It is about moving beyond what one has learned in order to achieve certain prescribed outcomes. It is about generating new knowledge and insights in a disciplined manner to obtain both the skilled capacity and a new mindset or paradigm for dealing with problems and issues in a continuous learning mode. This new mindset provides educators with the ability to welcome and engage in risks and the unknown, which is crucial to and preceeds the creation of new knowledge.

4. Ibid., 12.

6

Relationships

> "Educational change is a relationships-reframing process between those in the school and those outside the school."
>
> —*What's Worthy Fighting for Out There?, v–vi.*

ORGANIZATIONS SHOULD PAY EQUAL or more attention to the relational as well as the structural and statistical dimensions. Relationships and results are equally important. The issue here is how to shift leadership from being product-oriented to relationships-centered.

School District 2 in New York City served as an example of the type of relationships in the context of school district reform that were frequently cited to be emulated.[1] This reform was governed by an intensive professional development strategy led by several organizing principles. Professional development was also treated as an embedded and contextually independent variable that is part of the daily work of all administrative leaders, and not as an isolated component that is specialized or evoked at certain specific and assigned times. In this educational effort as well as others, several mechanisms were used to coordinate

1. Fullan, *Leading in a Culture of Change.*

relationships. These included monthly conferences, university partnerships, principal and staff meetings, videotaping, coaching, and interactive problem-solving sessions.

Finally, while relationships can be powerfully positive, they can also be powerfully negative.[2] Teachers' views and assumptions about learning and teaching can produce radically different cultures in the same school. Relationships function to color these assumptions. The presence of relationships does not automatically mean that they are focused on the right things. They may be misguided and/or further contribute to the problem that educational reform is to address in the first place. Some may contribute positively to student learning; others may not. What is required is for the leader to exercise his new role consistent with moral purpose and with a new mindset that says that he is there to create and nurture structures as well as relationships in which people can use their minds well to identify and generate new insights and to develop strategies for applying them.

How to help people cultivate these relationships is part of both the problem and the solution. It has been argued that what people need is emotional intelligence.[3] People should work on being street smart or on cultivating common sense. Emotional intelligence is something that can be learned. Leading in a culture of change is not only highly emotional, but also full of strong differences of opinion. Conflict is inevitable. Effective leadership take this resistance seriously. "Dissent is seen as a potential source of new ideas and breakthroughs."[4]

Relationships can make all the difference here. They can be used to accelerate and enhance the pace of educational

2. Ibid.
3. Ibid.
4. Ibid., 74.

change efforts and to navigate resulting and inevitable conflicts. Relationships are equally important to structure. They are nurtured by a caring, contextual, interdependent climate that is guided by moral purpose and high emotional intelligence.

7

Knowledge

"Educational change leaders work on changing
the context, helping create new settings condu-
cive to learning and sharing that learning."

—*Leading in a Culture of Change, 79.*

CREATING AND SHARING KNOWLEDGE fuels relationships.[1]
There is a clear difference between information and knowledge. "Information is machines. Knowledge is people."[2]
Information converts into knowledge as a result of collaboration and interaction. This is a social process. The use
and meaning of information is what ultimately counts. The
focus should be on the context and the individuals who will
be using that information, not solely on the information itself. "Leading in a culture of change does not mean placing
changed individuals into unchanged environments."[3]

Knowledge is tacit and explicit. It is tacit because it
is very individual. This can be personal information that
is not highly visible or easy to express. Knowledge is also
explicit because it is information that could be easily

1. Ibid.
2. Ibid., 78.
3. Ibid., 79.

communicated or disseminated in the traditional form of data and information. Success is associated with those organizations that have the capacity to access tacit knowledge. This is not easy to obtain because it should be sought first, sorted out, and then retained to be shared and used.

There is a direct relationship between creating and sharing knowledge and internal commitment.[4] In order to generate knowledge, a collaborative culture needs to be nurtured and sustained. Human interaction is crucial. Thus, the emotional lives of people are to be taken seriously. Knowledge sharing is important to creating a collaborative culture. Receiving and sharing knowledge is both a responsibility and opportunity. High performance organizations establish mechanisms whereby they reward and value the receiving and giving of information. Knowledge sharing and activation is not mandatory or controlling. Rather, it is a process whereby the organizational members become more energetic and inspired to contribute to organizational performance.

Knowledge sharing must be named a core value. Clear procedures and opportunities should be established for knowledge to be shared. The role of leaders in the knowledge creation and sharing business is not only to create opportunities or activities, but also to establish acceptable norms for the discussion and personally leading the process. Inter-visitation, peer networks, and instructional consulting services were some of the mechanisms implemented in educational reform efforts in New York City District 2 (mentioned previously) to create and share knowledge. It is important to point out that schools need to become cultures that create and share knowledge. Schools must start by naming this as a core value and then by finding ways to explicitly tackle the enormous cultural and structural barriers that handicap their capacity to share ideas and insights.

4. Ibid.

8

Sustainability

"Sustainability is the capacity of a system to engage in the complexities of continuous improvement consistent with deep values of human purpose."

—Leadership and Sustainability:
System Thinkers in Action, ix.

SUSTAINABILITY IS NOT CONCERNED with a particular educational initiative. Sustainability is concerned with the system, not system thinking. The challenge is how to develop and sustain a great number of system thinkers in action.[1] This is what is called the new theoretician. In an era of ever-increasing demands for performance and public accountability, it is understandable that institutions are expected to have improvements. However, whether those improvements are deep and lasting is the crux of the matter. What will it take for leaders and agencies to venture out into the unknown to discover and experiment with strategies that can take them beyond initial improvements? The

1. Michael Fullan, *Leadership and Sustainability: System Thinkers in Action* (Thousand Oaks, Ca.: Corwin, 2005).

main issue here is how to "pursue long-term sustainability without jeopardizing short-term results."[2]

Several years ago England's NLNS large-scale reform was somehow celebrated for the achievement of literacy and math targets. However, it was also worthy of critical attention due to the following reasons. First, only a minority of schools were able to engage deeply in these strategies, a fact that raises the issue of the moral purpose of closing the achievement gap. Second, the results remained stable, or flat-lined. Finally, the results did not point to sustainable reform and deep learning, and the initiative looked too centrally driven.

Moving beyond the initial plateau into sustainability requires informed, professional judgment, but this must be collective rather than an isolated and individual exercise. It is also crucial to interact with the wider environment of knowledge, not just with the inner world of the school. The problem here is that the school does not have the required resources for investing in capacity for informed professional judgments and therefore may drift into uninformed judgments. This dilemma is what sustainability is supposed to address.

The temptation of large-scale reform is to choose the wrong strategy and adopt lessons from apparent success. The danger in large-scale reform is thinking or concluding that either top-down or bottom-up is the answer to the problem. Large-scale reform suffers from two problems. One is that tacit and contextual knowledge must be taken into account. The other is that there is tremendous difficulty in knowing whether the model can work on a large, sustainable scale. What instead is needed is to recognize that building capacity is the answer. No Child Left Behind, the US reform act, and whole-school reform models

2. Ibid., x.

represented examples of initiatives that signal incomplete scenarios for sustainable reform due to the absence of investment capacity building.

There are eight elements of sustainability.[3] These include public service with a moral purpose; commitment to changing context at all levels; lateral capacity building through networks; intelligent accountability and vertical relationships (encompassing both capacity building and accountability); deep learning; dual commitment to short-term and long-term goals; cyclical energizing; and the long lever of leadership. Moral purpose must convert itself from an individual entity into an organizational and systemic quality. Commitment to changing contexts at all levels is about employing strategies that will alter and/or change the contexts under which people work. Collaboration is crucial for lateral capacity building through networks. Self-evaluation combined with a focused external inspection could be adopted as a strategy that can yield accountability and capacity results. Deep learning refers to the adaptive orientation and ability that organizations should have in order to deal with ever-increasing complex challenges and demands. For dual commitment to short and long-term results, a virtuous cycle should be created whereby public education delivers results, and the public, after gaining confidence, is able to invest more resources. Cyclical energizing, by implication, says that implementation is not linear, but cyclical. Energy levels (under use and over use) should be monitored. In addition, sustainability is cyclical because after higher rates of achievement in literacy and math, it has been found that there is a plateau. This is because the initial strategies that brought results cannot now bring further results. This is why cyclical energizing is valuable and crucial for sustainability.

3. Ibid.

Finally, sustainability requires leadership at all levels, albeit a different kind of leader, a leader that is able to think and act at the same time—systems thinkers in action or the new theoreticians.[4] This leadership needed for sustainability is not based on charismatic authority. The leader's performance is not defined by the result of students' achievements, but by the number of leaders that he leaves behind who can continue and deepen the work. The discontinuity of direction and the shortage of principals who are prepared to take on the sustainability agenda and the leadership qualities of prospective principals represent huge challenges.

How do individual leaders keep going without burning out? Leaders should revisit their moral purpose, be emotionally intelligent, mobilize positive sources of energy, avoid negative actions, and cease acting as pacesetters.[5] The key here is to have a balanced view of energy. Energy is not to be over used or under used. Individual leaders need to be more energy creators rather than energy neutrals and consumers. Leaders also need energy recovery, whether in rituals or periods of solitude. The individual focus should be accompanied by an explicit focus on changing systems. The development of systems of thinkers is the key. It is about developing people that will engage in strategies that will change people's system-related experiences.

Leaders in the sustainability business must be able to discriminate between technical and adaptive solutions and between progressive and regressive interactions when dealing with complex problems and exchanging ideas and knowledge. They also need to employ different languages if they expect transformation to take place. There is a strong need for leaders to both explain and act in ways that will

4. Ibid.
5. Ibid.

lead to system transformation. Leaders do not only start the process; they also keep it going. Leaders act locally and globally.

At the school level, leadership must tackle both technical and adaptive problems. Leaders are called to design educational atmospheres intentionally directed at engaging teachers in the discussion of student work (assessment for learning), changing the school cultures (through professional development capacity-building strategies), and engaging educators and communities in a genuine dialogue and action steps about what to do to improve the conditions of schools, students, and parents.

At the district level, a set of preconditions must be present for sustainability. These include "leading with a compelling, driving conceptualization; collective moral purpose; the right bus; capacity-building; lateral capacity-building; ongoing learning; productive conflict; a demanding culture; external partners and growing financial investments."[6] At the system level, the leader should both be working toward coherence and horizontal and vertical interactions to promote system thinking. System leaders are urged to follow ten guidelines: "the reality test," or putting into practice system thinking; "moral purpose," which must be made a systemic quality; getting "the basics right," which is building deep learning in literacy and numeracy; communicating "the big picture," opportunities for locals to influence the big picture; "intelligent accountability," examining what is working best; "incentivize collaboration and capacity-building," establishing clear expectations for intra-organizational professional interaction; "the long lever of leadership," or, leaders whose legacy is leaving leaders behind them who can continue and deepen the work; and designing "every policy, whatever the pur-

6. Ibid., 66.

pose, to build capacity and grow the financial investment in education"—sustainability needs and produces new resources.[7]

Developing and sustaining a great number of system thinkers in action is the key. Sustainability depends on leaders who are both thinkers and doers. It relies and thrives on leaders who act locally and globally as well as on those who are concerned with the small and big pictures. Leadership that feeds sustainability is concerned with both short and long-term goals. One is not sacrificed at the expense of the other. The work of the new leader for sustainability is not only to have a balanced or combined approach or to reconcile these dilemmas, but to plan and prepare for succession, to know how to gain, release, and recover energy, and to engage in and deliberate strategies explicitly tailored to change schools, districts, and systems.

7. Ibid., 84–98.

9

Chaos/Complexity and Evolutionary Theories

> "You cannot get to new horizons without grasping the essence of complexity theory. The trick is to learn to become a tad more comfortable with the awful mystery of complex systems, to do fewer things to aggravate what is already a centrifugal problem, resist controlling the uncontrollable, and to learn to use the key complexity concepts to design and guide more powerful systems. You need to tweak and trust the process of change while knowing that it is unpredictable."
>
> —*Change Forces with a Vengeance*, 21.

CHAOS/COMPLEXITY AND EVOLUTIONARY THEORY can help us unpack what it means to have productive educational change. First, chaos/complexity theory claims that the link between cause and effect is difficult to trace, that change (planned and otherwise) unfolds in nonlinear ways, that paradoxes and contradictions abound, and that creative solutions arise out of the interaction under conditions of uncertainty, diversity, and instability.[1] Chaos/complex-

---

1. Fullan, *Change Forces: The Sequel*, 4.

ity theory is about learning and adapting to changing and uncertain circumstances.

As a result, information that becomes knowledge is not an event and does not reside in a single entity. It is a process. It has a relational dimension. Thus, knowledge is found in communities of practice. These communities of practice (professional learning communities of teachers and principals acting together) do not only produce knowledge but also actionable strategies for utilizing that knowledge. This knowledge is to be produced and shared. The power of chaos/complexity theory for organizational learning rests in the fact that there must be an ongoing interaction where people are producing and discovering knowledge while at the same time taking ownership and questioning each other.[2]

Perhaps the greatest challenge of chaos/complexity theory insights is how to expect true outcomes when the system is nonlinear. The response to this incisive concern is that the strategies used in a school system should be looked upon not only as the engine behind meeting short-term results, but also as to whether it increases and decreases people's energy and motivation without which there cannot be long-term continuous improvement. Since chaos/complexity theories predict conflict amid interaction, it leads toward greater discipline compared to a hierarchical and mechanistic system, which provides no space for the disagreement and discussion of new meanings and ideas.

Evolutionary theory "raises the questions of how humans evolve over time, especially in relation to interaction and cooperative behavior."[3] Mature humans are known for evolving from the self-centered to a more cooperative behavior. Thus, collaboration is the key. Interaction is a ne-

2. Fullan, *The Moral Imperative of School Leadership*.

3. Fullan, *Change Forces: The Sequel*, 6.

cessity because teachers need each other's knowledge. Thus, evolutionary theory can serve higher moral purposes. Its underlying practical interaction component can produce social cohesion. Interaction can help us solve problems. Its diversity and resulting conflict can help us find solutions to problems for which no easy answers exist, especially in this age of rapid change.

The basic message of chaos/complexity and evolutionary theories is that educators and leaders should learn to live with change. There is a need for an understanding of balance. There should not be too much control because it undermines professional autonomy and discretion. However, there should not be too much freedom because it can lead to license and disorder. These theories also tell us that interactions are needed for creating and sharing knowledge and for the triggering of moral purpose and the self-organized filters that can produce and sustain a learning organization.

10

Systems

> "Educational transformation will require changes (new capacities) within each of the three levels and across their relationships. The levels are: the school, the district and the state."
>
> —*Change Forces with a Vengeance, 39.*

EDUCATIONAL TRANSFORMATION WILL NOT take place unless capacity-building results are attained at three levels: the school, the district, and the state.[1] Significant interaction is required and expected across and within each of these levels if capacities are to be enhanced. The tri-level argument says that "each layer is helped or hindered by the layer above it (and each layer needs the commitment and energies of other layers in order to be successful)."[2]

Recent successful educational reforms lack depth. They do not have the capacities to engage in powerful learning that is lasting, continuous, and sustainable. Gaining people's commitments and increasing their capacities in large school systems is the central issue. The response is the tri-level capacity development of school, district, and state.

1. Fullan, *The Moral Imperative of School Leadership.*
2. Ibid., 52.

At the school level, teachers and principals can start by working together inside their schools and by linking to external parties. Teachers and principals can start by building and nurturing professional communities. They can also start by involving parents and engaging with local and regional partnerships. It is a great mistake to treat schools as if they are islands. They are part of a larger picture which is the district. It is also a great mistake to confuse theories of education with theories of change. "A theory of education includes the substance of content and pedagogy."[3] A theory of change or action "concerns what policies, strategies and mechanisms are going to be used, in effect, to implement the theory of education."[4] They represent the difference between deep and/or superficial change.

The role of the district level is to be wary of external models and pacesetting leaders. The role of the district includes the following: taking into account the energy and intrinsic motivation and commitment of teachers; adopting a balanced and combined approach of capacity building and accountability strategies; ensuring that teachers internalize the core underlying conceptions that produce powerful and deep learning; providing greater coherence and alignment among policies; and monitoring the improvement that results from strategies as they unfold. The point here is that if the reform cannot be sustained beyond initial results, then it is not successful at all.

At the state level, policymakers and politicians should heed the following eight lessons: "Give up the idea that change will slow down; coherence-making is everyone's responsibility; changing in conditions is priority; respond to the public thirst for transparency; use large-scale reform strategies but beware of the trap of teacher dependency or

3. Ibid.
4. Ibid., 53.

alienation; convert teacher, principal and district skepticism into commitment and ownership and as you focus on leadership development as key, and don't take shortcuts."[5]

In addition, the state should also align curriculum, assessment, and teacher learning policies and unite them to moral purpose and to the creation and sharing of knowledge.[6] The efficacy of this model should be measured by the teacher passion, purpose, and capacity that is created as well as by the student engagement and learning that is generated. This tri-level argument is a concern for system change. It is a humble proposition that one part cannot be (or stay) reformed without other parts. Hence, the basic message of the tri-level argument is that educational change is a multilevel (school, district, and state) capacity-building process.

5. Ibid., 66–68.
6. Ibid.

1 1

Paradoxes

"Educational change is the constant search for understanding, knowing there is no ultimate answer."

—*Change Forces: Proving the Depths of Educational Reform, 20.*

THE NEW LANGUAGE FOR educational change is paradoxical in nature. Educational change faces four major paradoxes. There are also various lessons (mini paradoxes) that derive from these major paradoxes. Paradoxes explain best the new mindset, paradigm, or worldview that governs our knowledge society. They demand a different kind of thinking. They turn traditional thinking about organizational development, learning, and transformation on its head. They require us to revise and reverse our assumptions and adopt truths sensitive to the times that we live in.

Rather than focusing on the rational and the structural, the focus now is on reculturing and strategizing for a complex system. This in itself is contradictory or paradoxical because it is hard to understand how stability and coherence are to be gained in what is indefinitely an unstable and incoherent world with a relentless pace of change. The first paradox is: "Transformation would not be possible without accompanying messiness."[1]

How learning and capacity building (a slow process) takes place in a time of rapid change represents the second major paradox. Rapid change demands "slow learning in context over time."[2] The third major paradox is how continuous change is to be provided alongside a continuously conservative system.[3] Finally, the fourth major paradox is how one brings about system transformation (the result of a collective effort) in a system that is heavily individualistic.

Basically, the aim of educational change is to reconcile opposites. Fullan describes the eight lessons that result from the new paradigm of educational change.[4] These include the following: "you can't mandate what matters"; "change is a journey not a blueprint"; "problems are our friends"; "vision and strategic planning come later"; "individualism and collectivism must have equal power"; "neither centralization nor decentralization works"; "connection with the wider environment is critical for success"; and "every person is a change agent."[5] Complex change can be best described by eight lessons. These are as follows: "moral purpose is complex and problematic"; "theories of change and theories of education need each other"; "conflict and diversity are our friends"; "understand the meaning of operating on the edge of chaos"; "emotional intelligence is anxiety provoking and anxiety containing"; "collaborative cultures are anxiety provoking and anxiety containing"; "attack incoherence: connections and knowledge creation

1. Fullan, *Leading in a Culture of Change*, 31.
2. Ibid., 121.
3. Fullan, *Change Forces*, 3.
4. Ibid.
5. Ibid., 21–22.

are critical"; and "there is no single solution: craft your own theories and actions by being a critical consumer."[6]

Educational change is full of paradoxes. It must be. The presence and challenges that face institutions that operate under modernistic assumptions in what is without a doubt an increasingly postmodern society makes this inevitable and predictable.

6. Michael Fullan, *Change Forces: The Sequel* (Bristol, Pa.: Falmer, 1999), 18.

12

Coherence

"Coherence doesn't happen by accident, and doesn't happen by pursuing everything under the sun. Effective organizations are not ones that innovate the most; they are not ones that send personnel on the most number of staff development conferences. No, they are organizations that selectively go about learning more. In all of their activities, even ones that foster diversity, they create mechanisms of integration. Moral purpose, communication, intense interaction, implementation plans, performance data all serve the purpose of coherence. In examining new policies or possibilities integrative organizations not only weigh the value of each opportunity, by they also ask how the idea 'connects' with what they are doing. Shared meaning and organizational connectedness are the long-term assets of high performing systems."

—*Change Forces: The Sequel, 28.*

WE LIVE IN A chaotic society. This means that we live in a state of fragmentation and overload. This condition pushes us to seek new ideas and insights. These can be generated especially under chaotic conditions when the present status quo is disrupted. However, this can also result if anarchy is not looked at or treated properly. Creating coherence is sorely needed to make sense of and take advantage of this chaotic and complex state.

Schools face the problem of having too many uncoordinated and imposed policies that lead to innovations that are superficially implemented. School leaders need to act in ways that will produce results. There is a strong need for adaptive leadership.[1] Educational leaders need to adopt a process and ideas that can help them gain widespread support and internal commitment from those below in the hierarchy.

Two concepts of complexity science relate to creating coherence.[2] One is self-organizing, and the other is strange attractors. The first one refers to the new patterns and relationships that are formed when moral purpose and knowledge sharing is used in combination with knowledge of the change process and relationships. The second refers to elements that help you gain the commitment and energy of those below in the hierarchy. An example of strange attractors is visions.

Leaders working on creating coherence establish clear expectations and/or goals and then design a process to pursue them. This process of pursuing goals creates great disturbance and conflict. However, in the end, this process not only ends up with self-organizing patterns but also with strange attractors. Leaders must be able to work through the uncertainties of a culture shaped by complex problems.

One of the ideas used to build coherence is assessment literacy. This capacity-building practice is one in which the principal and the teachers, in order to reach certain specific outcomes, meet together to look at and disaggregate

1. Fullan, *Leading in a Culture of Change*, 110.
2. Ibid.

data, to develop further action plans, and to talk about the public debate concerning the value and uses of data in an assessment-driven era.

Leaders are respectful and mindful of the messiness that accompanies chaotic and complex environments. Creating coherence has three features: "lateral accountability"; "the sorting process embedded in knowledge-creation and knowledge-sharing"; and the shared commitments to selected ideas and paths of action.[3]

3. Ibid., 118.

13

Theory of Action

"Give me a good theory over a strategic plan
any day of the week. A plan is a tool—a piece of
technology only as good as the mind-set using
it. The mind-set is theory, flawed or otherwise.
Theory is not abstract conjecture, and it is not
about being cerebral. . . . Theories, in other
words, make sense of the real world and are test-
ed against it. The best theories are at their core
solidly grounded in action. Theories that travel
well are those that practically and insightfully
guide the understanding of complex situations
and point to actions likely to be effective under
the circumstances. Good theories travel across
sectors of public and private organizations, and
they apply to geographically and culturally diverse situations."

—*The Six Secrets of Change, 1.*

DUE TO THE CLAIM that the "world has become too complex for any theory to have certainty,"[1] traveling with good

1. Michael Fullan, *The Six Secrets of Change: What the Best Leaders Do to Help Their Organizations Survive and Thrive* (San Francisco,
Ca.: Jossey-Bass, 2008), 5.

theory is recommended. Examples of good theory that travel are evolutionary theory (mentioned earlier) and former head of Tony Blair's Prime Minister Delivery Unit, Michael Barber's (2007) theory of action, which includes "ambitious goals, sharp focus, clarity and transparency of data and a relentless sense of urgency."[2] Bringing about deep and lasting change in organizations demands that leaders master six secrets: love your employees; connect peers with purpose; capacity building prevails; learning is the work; transparency rules; and systems rule. Five assumptions and criteria that underpin these secrets are that they are large-scale; understood to be synergistic; heavily nuanced; motivationally embedded; and represent a tension or dilemma. All types of leaders are called to practice these secrets. Surviving and thriving in the twenty-first century entails following several guidelines in order to keep the secrets: "Seize the energy, define your own traveling theory, share a secret, keep a secret; the world is the only oyster you have, stay on the far side of complexity and happiness is not what some of us think."[3] Cultivating these six secrets will help people find their purpose in life—the bottom line.

2. Ibid., 9.
3. Ibid., 123.

Summary

THIS SHORT BOOK HAS attempted to describe key operational concepts that undergird theories of educational change. This text underscores some foundational themes in the work of one of the authorities in the rapidly growing field of educational change as it deals with different actors in education as well as various concepts describing theoretical data. No single stakeholder is excluded. Every one of these is examined in relation to educational change. A closer and more detailed look at these works reveals a strong tendency in the educational change literature to focus on adults rather than students and on the system rather than a specific unit. At the same time, works described and examined here are full of terms that convey theoretical ideas and concepts aimed at redefining and reframing educational change and reform in terms of not only individual and structural conditions, but also collective and cultural aspects of organizations—in this case, schools and district systems. While this dual focus and approach is quite inclusive and therefore to be welcomed, valued, and appreciated, the lack of depth particularly on such stakeholders as students or the absence of an approach to deal with power, politics, and diversity may be a clarion call and an invitation to embark on a research journey that allows for a more direct, substantial, and rich analysis of such stakeholders and issues. *Enduring Themes in Educational Change* is a noble and humble call towards that quest.

References

BELOW ARE REFERENCES FOR major themes listed in order of year published.

Fullan, M. *The New Meaning of Educational Change.* First edition. New York: Teachers College Press, 1982.

———. *The New Meaning of Educational Change.* Second edition. New York: Teachers College Press, 1991.

———, and A. Hargreaves. *Understanding Teacher Development.* New York: Teachers College Press, 1992.

———, and A. Hargreaves. *What's Worth Fighting for in Your School?.* New York: Teachers College Press, 1992.

———. *Successful School Improvement.* Buckingham: Open University Press, 1992.

———. *Change Forces: Probing the Depths of Educational Reform.* London: Falmer, 1993.

———. *What's Worth Fighting for in the Principalship?.* First edition. New York: Teachers College Press, 1997.

———, and A. Hargreaves. *What's Worth Fighting for Out There?.* New York: Teachers College Press, 1998.

———. *Change Forces: The Sequel.* Bristol, Pa.: Falmer, 1999.

———. *Leading in a Culture of Change.* San Francisco: Jossey-Bass, 2001.

———. *The New Meaning of Educational Change.* Third edition. New York: Teachers College Press, 2001.

———. *Change Forces with a Vengeance.* London: Routledge Falmer, 2003.

REFERENCES

————. *The Moral Imperative of School Leadership*. Thousand Oaks, Ca.: Corwin, 2003.

————. *Leadership and Sustainability: System Thinkers in Action*. Thousand Oaks, Ca.: Corwin, 2005.

————. *The Six Secrets of Change: What the Best Leaders Do to Help Their Organizations Survive and Thrive*. San Francisco, Ca.: Jossey-Bass, 2008.

————. *What's Worth Fighting for in the Principalship?*. Second edition. New York: Teachers College Press, 2008.